The
Ten Irrefutable Laws
of Horsemanship

The
Ten Irrefutable Laws
of Horsemanship

by

Geoff Tucker, DVM

ISBN 978-0-557-57323-3

Contents

Introduction vii

Law 1   A Horse Can Hurt You & Even Kill You 1

Law 2   The Horse That Can Kill You Is Your
Own 3

Law 3   When doing anything with a horse,
always use a halter and lead rope. Stay
connected. 5

Law 4   Always Place Yourself Between The
Horse And The Exit 9

Law 5   Become The Leader 11

Law 6   To Be The Leader Of Horses You Need
To Know The Personalities Of Horses 13

Law 7   Seek First To Understand 17

Law 8   Then To Be Understood 21

Law 9   The Law Of Energy 23

Law 10 A Horse Is A Horse 27

Conclusion 31

Bibliography 33

<u>INTRODUCTION</u>

An irrefutable law is impossible to deny or disprove. Many say laws are meant to be broken. A plane defies the law of gravity by flying. But the law of gravity always wins at the end of the day.

We look at laws more as an inconvenience when in reality, the laws of this earth are never broken. For the plane, the law of lift becomes stronger than the law of gravity. We outsmart gravity - until lift is gone and then gravity once again rules.

In the horse world there are laws as well. Often we try to break them and with disastrous consequences.

This short book is for all who work with horses. Everyone. Because these laws apply to anyone who gets near a horse. The nation you live in and the language you speak has no bearing on how these laws apply.

For the person who is new to horses, learn these laws and apply them. You will live long and without serious injury. Many of you are supplemental to the ownership of the horse. Basically you are the bill payer. But you will need to learn these laws as well as discuss them with your children. You have a responsibility to them for their safety. Experienced horse owners may have developed a system without these laws that works for them. Years have passed without a problem. But like the plane that loses lift, you too will lose to these broken laws.

Prevention is far easier. Preparing in your mind and turning prepared actions into habits will diminish your chances of injury. It is in the mind where you need to start. A helmet secured to your head will prevent many injuries. But paying attention to and connecting to your horse at all times will diminish the action that causes the wreck in the first place.

Why is this book so important? Simply put, our relationship with horses has changed. For the majority of people in the US, horses are recreational vehicles parked in the garage and pulled out on weekends or maybe an hour at the end of the work day. No longer are horses an integral part of life where 12 hours a day were spent with horses. In fact many owners show up just to ride while a hired hand does all the work.

The connection between man and horse is rarely made which makes the following rules even more important.

At first the rules will appear restrictive, but they are not. Once they become habit, they will be second nature. They may save your life or your horse's life.

LAW #1 - A HORSE CAN HURT YOU & EVEN KILL YOU

The reason this is the first law is because I have seen many horse owners be clueless about the fact that these beautiful animals weigh 5 to 10 times more than we do.

Let me ask this. Would you allow me to swing a baseball bat at your head? A horse's leg has more weight and moves as fast as a swinging bat. Their hooves can fracture bones as well as organs that can cause you to bleed internally.

Here's another question. Would you let me run into you as fast as I can? Even if we were equal in weight, my mass times speed will hurt you. Now imagine 10 of me running into you at the same time. No question you would be hurt.

Yes, the 1st law is to be aware that a horse can kill you. Usually it is an inadvertent act, not a direct act. "He was kicking at a fly and I was in the way." has been said too many times. Why were you standing behind the horse?

There have been outright attacks by horses I call "FELONS." I have permanent scars from two separate unprovoked attacks.

Then there are the accidents when with apparently no warning something happens. Once I was working on an anesthetized foal and while it was asleep on it's side it kicked me. Couldn't predict that! Another time I was passing a stomach tube up the nose of a mare and she stepped forward with her hoof onto the tip of my shoe. My toes were OK but my foot was pinned to the floor. Her body moved forward into me. Because my foot was pinned, I started to fall as I was pushed. All would have been OK, but my rib met the corner of a wooden box feeder and it broke my rib. Any other spot in the stall and I would have been OK.

On memorial Day, 2008, my friend, colleague, and original veterinary mentor was working with a horse. He had been an equine vet for more than 40 years. Somehow this horse knocked him to the ground causing a head injury causing his death 3 days later.

A horse can hurt you and even kill you. Please remember this - always.

LAW #2 - THE HORSE THAT CAN KILL YOU IS YOUR OWN

This law brings it home. Often I see people be cautious around a strange horse. Yet around their own the tragedy strikes.

If we all agree with law #1, why do we think it doesn't apply to us and our own horses?

Almost every person I know either hurt or killed by a horse has been caused by a familiar horse. Kicked while grooming or feeding or falling off a horse that was walking.

This last example came true for a friend of mine, a professional riding instructor, riding her horse back to the barn on the buckle. Her horse tripped and she landed on her head killing her in 15 minutes.

Yes, accidents do happen all the time around horses. The more you are with them the more chance you have of getting hurt. Always be aware of your horse and your surroundings to minimize your risks of injury. ANY horse can hurt you and even cause your death. In today's world where impairment by distractions while driving causes more accidents and deaths, consider the unpredictability of the living horse and not being tuned into the horse and the surroundings. Only a moment and you or your horse - your favorite, best friend of a horse - can become a statistic.

With all of this doom and gloom, I still work daily with horses. I am not afraid even though I have been hurt several times in the past. Why? Because the connection made with the horse is SO worth it. It is the only reason that after being with horses since 1973 and as a vet since 1984 I still look forward to the connection with each horse I work with today.

My point is simply this: if the connection is the juice of being with a horse, why cast it aside when you are with them? It is what makes being with a horse FUN! It is also the loss of this connection that causes trouble.

The remaining laws deal with minimizing the risks. Use them to favor you in preventing injury & pain.

LAW #3 – WHEN DOING ANYTHING WITH A HORSE, ALWAYS USE A HALTER AND LEAD ROPE. STAY CONNECTED.

Mechanical Advantage is a physics principle dealing with leverage. In simple terms, a lever allows you to multiply your strength.

When a horse wants to go in a direction other than where you want it to go, you need to turn it's head only for the body to follow. The head is attached to a very long and strong neck.

When the head and neck turn and you get *behind* this movement, you have lost control of the horse. However, if you are attached directly to the head with a length of rope where your closest hand to the horse is about 2 feet away, then the leverage you can apply to the head can overcome the strength of the neck. Control can quickly and easily be returned to the handler.

When the length of the rope between the horse and the hand becomes longer than 2 feet, the leverage is lost because again the horse can get ahead of you. In addition, with too long a lead the horse can actually kick you.

When you lead a horse or work around him, keep the the lead near this 2 foot mark. This will keep you in the safety zone next to his shoulder. Here a horse will have difficulty striking or kicking you, though it is still possible to do both.

Keep yourself connected to the horse even if you need to move further than 2 feet. For example, when you need to work around the back end of a horse you can allow the lead to lengthen. If the horse spooks, he will come up short and bring his attention back to you where it belongs. If you are not attached, he is gone creating the potential for injury. A better approach is to have someone else hold the horse. That person should always remain on the same side of the horse that you are working on.

If alone and the horse ties, then use this to keep control.

I have seen people use halters without a lead or even lead a horse with only a handful of mane. These people have developed bad habits that will eventually cause injury. In addition, this teaches bad habits to young people watching. And they are always watching!

If you are new to horses, learn the proper way to stay physically connected to your horse. For those taking shortcuts, I realize you may have a good track record and your horse will never hurt you. Be beware of this: we are always teaching someone who is watching us. Those people then purchase a new horse that does not have the manners of your horse. The new owner uses your poor habits of leading or working around the horse and subsequently one of them gets hurt. You are to blame.

Take the time. Don't be lazy. Do it right every time. Set the example.

LAW #4 - ALWAYS PLACE YOURSELF BETWEEN THE HORSE AND THE EXIT

This location always needs to be in your head. There is nothing worse than to be in the back of the stall especially when LAW #3 has been broken & there is nothing connecting you to the horse. If the door is open, the horse will usually leave. But if the door is closed and the horse is upset, then you could end up pressed between his hind hooves and the stall wall.

But I know, this won't happen to you because your horse loves you. So lets take a look at another situation - turning your horse out into the paddock.

Do you lead the horse through the paddock gate, turn him loose, then slap him on the butt as he goes by? If so, you may become a statistic when he kicks out as he goes by.

The correct safe way to turn out is to walk through the gate, turn the horse around and have him face you. Now you are between the exit and the horse. Before letting go, have the horse reach a clam state. When he is calm release the horse and start walking *away* from the horse through the gate and close it.

Releasing a horse that is not calm and allowing him to run away from you is not respectful, dangerous and promotes anarchy in the herd. **This is a loss of your leadership position**. From this point everything else proceeds downhill.

Placing yourself between the horse and the exit places you in control and keeps you safe.

LAW #5 - BECOME THE LEADER

Horses live in a herd world with an organization of one boss and the rest. You are part of that herd. If you won't be the leader, the horse will.

The horse has a brain that is similar to ours. Think of my Mac computer and your Windows computer - both do basically the same thing but each use a different operating system. Similarly, our operating system is different than a horse.

Both our brains have a neocortex about the size of a dinner napkin and as thick as 3 business cards stacked together. It covers the outside of the brain and is the source of all our memories and thoughts. I am going to assume that because our neocortex and the horses neocortex are so similar, we can have similar thoughts, memories and personalities. However, because of the different operating systems, our structure of important life issues are different.

We can all agree that when a new born baby or foal gets hungry, they are both wired to nurse. After that, things differ. The foal gets up and starts to run, his first step to becoming part of the herd. The infant on the other hand seems to crawl forever and becomes dependent on the family unit.

In the herd dynamic, there is a hierarchy, also known as a pecking order. Foals don't read a book on this. It just is. Each foal compares itself to those around it, then based on it's wiring plus life experiences, either settles for where he is, allows himself to be placed at the bottom of the heap, or fights for top position.

It is important to realize that you are part of this herd positioning.

Does your horse follow you everywhere or does he stay far away? When you ask him for something, is his answer "yes", "no" or "maybe"? Does he snap to attention or does he ignore you or disrespect you?

If your relationship with your horse places you at least equal or better, then your life with horses will be good. But if your horse has become the leader and runs rough shod over you then at best your life with horses will be miserable and at worst, you may become injured. Unless of course it is not in you to be a leader. If that is the case, then it is best for you to find the horse who also doesn't want to be the leader. You will both be very happy.

LAW #6 - TO BE THE LEADER OF HORSES YOU NEED TO KNOW THE PERSONALITIES OF HORSES

Socrates thought, almost 2000 years ago, that our personalities came from our body fluids. He named them *Sanguine*, *Melancholy*, *Choleric* and *Phlegmatic*. I will briefly describe them here but you can read more from hundreds of books written about this. My favorite is <u>*Personality Plus*</u> by Florence Littauer.

Before I describe the personality types you need to know 2 things. First - we are blends of these with one or two being dominant. Ideally we should be an equal blend. Second - because I have worked with over 44,000 horses, I have seen these same basic personalities types in horses.

<u>Sanguine</u> - the life of the party, loves attention, loves the spotlight, fun to be around, makes friends easily, energetic, emotional, loves people, charming.

<u>Choleric</u> - demanding, dominant, strong willed, independent, confident, goal oriented, good under pressure, loves the competition.

<u>Melancholy</u> - organized, orderly, thinkers, analytical, artistic, perfectionist, needs to complete things, avoids attention, faithful, compassionate.

<u>Phlegmatic</u> - Low keyed, easy going, doesn't get flustered, takes his time, peaceful, everyone likes him, balanced but hides emotions.

Have I described your horse? In my business I need to know what the dominant personality of the horse is as soon as I enter the stall. 9 times out of 10 it's easy.

Become good at this because your ability to communicate with your horse is proportional to your understanding of his personality.

For instance you would never say to a dominant choleric, "Excuse me, but would you like to walk with me out to the paddock?" His answer will always be determined by him and not you - "yes" if he wants to go, "no" if he doesn't want to, or "maybe" if he thinks there might be something in it for him but he needs to be sure first.

You best be on your game when you walk an excited sanguine out to the paddock because there will be much dancing.

Have fun learning these and play a game with your friends and family. Determine their personality then determine their horse's personality. Become good at this improving to the point of being confident in the shortest amount of time. Don't be frustrated if you don't get it right away especially when people cover up their true personalities or hide behind them. Luckily, the horse usually wears his personality on his sleeve. That's why we like them so much.

LAW #7 - SEEK FIRST TO UNDERSTAND

This is *part A* of the basic tool of communication.

Horses have become a part time endeavor for most horse owners in the United States. Like a recreational vehicle parked in a garage and brought out on weekends, horses have become objects. This isn't as bad as it sounds. When it goes wrong is when we don't take the time to listen to them. That is when they truly become an inanimate object - a very sad day in the life of a horse.

I know many of you love your horse and talk to them all the time, lavishing gifts of treats. But how many of you listen? What is more important, how many horses have stopped trying to tell you what you need to hear?

Here is an example. Pretend you cannot speak Chinese. Now pretend you are in a room of 1,000 Chinese people - and you need to go to the bathroom. As time passes your sense of urgency mounts, but everyone you ask doesn't speak your language and you don't speak theirs.

You have tears rolling down your face, your legs are crossed, your foot is tapping, you're embarrassed, you can't think of anything else, you are agitated, and you are starting to hate all people who don't speak your language.

There is no difference between not knowing a language and not listening - it is your choice. Just because a horse can not form or speak words doesn't mean he can't say something.

You are about to give up when a Chinese person who does not speak your language understands the "other" language of someone needing a bathroom. He takes your hand and leads you through the crowd to the bathroom.

Guess who just became your best friend? The one who sought first to understand you. You may be a Sanguine, Choleric, Melancholy, or Phlegmatic and the same with the person who helped you. Seeking to understand is universal and is not personality dependent. That comes next.

But in all communication - human or horse - there is always a starting point. If you want to become a leader of your horse, you have a choice. You can go in and demand action much like climbing into your recreational vehicle, starting the engine, and stomping on the gas. OR you can ask permission to enter the stall and ask simply, "How are you my friend?"

As the leader you set the tone. There is no better way to set the tone than to recognize that these are living, breathing animals with thoughts and personalities. This only takes a moment.

The words don't have to be said. Just offer your hand and let him sniff, rub the head, or touch the shoulder. STOP AND LISTEN, then ask, "Are you with me?"

You have established communication effectively by doing this. Believe me because I do this about 3500 times a year before I place a carbide steel file into their mouth and start filing the teeth. 9 out of 10 horses let me do this willingly without drugs or equipment.

LAW # 8 - THEN TO BE UNDERSTOOD

This is *part B* and is always applied after LAW 7 - SEEK FIRST TO UNDERSTAND.

You are the leader of your horse every moment you are with him. Now that you have established an open and willing line of communication and determined that your horse is willing to listen, you need to select the form or style of communication. This is where understanding their personalities comes in.

A larger body of work may be needed here, but the basics are simple. A point needs to be made first. Just because a horse cannot speak human languages doesn't mean he can't understand your words. A case in point is your dog. "Come, sit, stay, roll over, play dead" are all human words your dog understands. Another case in point is saying things to an infant. So use words effectively when working with your horse and stop calling him "BUTT HEAD"!

When you want a horse with a dominant personality to do something:

Sanguine - make it fun, congratulate abundantly, smile, laugh, but don't expect them to follow orders. Guide gently.

Choleric - make it his idea, use language like you were talking to a human, be confident, show him that he can do it and that he wants to do it, work together and allow him leadership in the task while offering confidence and guidance, constantly communicate ideas but stop nagging him - he gets it already.

Melancholy - Be organized, stick to the plan, be proactive, if anything changes (a bird suddenly flies up) stick to the plan or adapt and maintain your direction. These guys follow orders well and are focused but be clear and detailed. Vagueness doesn't work.

Phlegmatic - remain the rock of confidence he needs, never sway, be the decision maker. He will always forgive you and he will save your butt when you get into trouble. These horses become the "bomb proof" ones.

LAW #9 - THE LAW OF ENERGY

Never exceed the energy of the horse. Leadership never comes from a higher level of energy.

Think of every leader you have known - real or in the movies - they are calm and confident. Clint Eastwood as Dirty Harry - "Go ahead make my day." I also know that only a few people can actually lower their energy levels on demand and rarely in the face of high energy.

The first step is to recognize that you and whoever you are with have an energy level. When you are with someone you are comfortable with your energy level is low because of your confidence in your relationship with that person or situation.

Don't confuse excitement with a high energy level. This is best explained with an example. Think of when you are about to enter an event on your horse. The crowd is watching. Other horses are close by. You have worked hard and paid money to be here and it is all you have thought about all week. Both you and your horse are excited. As a leader, you must maintain a low energy level in the face of this excitement. This gives a sense of confidence and leadership to the horse that you know what you are doing.

A teacher is confident on the first day of class even though all the students are new. Don't confuse excitement with a high energy level. The teacher is in his element and is therefore confident. He automatically is the leader.

What happens when a student challenges that teacher's authority? The result is dependent upon the teacher's reaction to the student's elevated energy. Pretend you are the teacher and your horse is the student who is claiming the responsibility of leadership. Here are the various outcomes.

#1 You surrender the leadership role to the horse and he becomes the boss. He eats all day and you go in the house either wondering why you are wasting your money or worse, you are in an ambulance.

#2 No one surrenders the leadership. The horse raises his energy and you raise your energy to match. Then you up the energy level and the horse does the same. This is what I call a *crescendo* - a word which means that the music is growing louder.

Both the human and the horse think they are the leaders because each is increasing their energy trying to dominate each other. In reality there is anarchy.

Not only is there no leader, each party is a follower. After the battle there's a winner and a loser which is not a very good relationship. The possible results are the same for both the human and the horse: a) spirit is broken and/or b) bones are broken.

#3 You remain the leader. If leadership comes from the lowest energy level, from confidence, then as a leader you cannot raise your energy to the level of the horse. When your horse starts to scream "The sky is falling, the sky is falling!!!", a leader does not look at the sky. He does not crescendo. The leader only sees where the leader wants to be and leads the followers to that place.

When you feel energy levels rising, consciously bring your energy levels down.

LAW #10 - A HORSE IS A HORSE

This Law is so important to understand and is easily applied no matter what your personality is. Yet in my experience this simple thought seems so elusive because people live in a complex world. People become confused between the emotion they have being with horses and the fact that it is the _connection_ with the horse that brings the joy and not the physical horse.

If it was just the horse, then why do we cry when he dies? Logically you should be happy - one less stall to clean, less supplies to purchase. The reason we cry is because upon the death of the horse, we have lost the connection that means so much to us.

Before you read more, please let me explain. We all love horses, but it is our definition of love that we may not agree on. I know well the saying, "A way to a man's heart is through his stomach." When I first met my wife she cooked up a storm. Now 33 years later, it is not the cooking that has kept us together. It is the CONNECTION. It is the conversation we have while we eat or the fun we have trying a new restaurant.

Nurturing the connection of who we are, not who we think the other should be is what has worked for us. Same with your horse. Don't try to change him into something he can never be. Your horse is not a surrogate child, a surrogate spouse, therapy for your problems at work, the friend you cannot find in the people world, a cow, dog, cat, or any other animal.

Take the horse for what he is - an individual living being with certain needs and desires unique to the horse.

You were a child once. Did your parent greet you in the afternoon after school with a bowl of candy then ask if you wouldn't mind cleaning your room and possibly do a little school work? No! Then why is it OK to greet your horse with carrots, candies, and treats and then ask if he might want to do a little work?

Why do we feed horses "meals" when they are continuous eaters as evidenced by being one of the few animals I know that has no gall bladder? They can not store bile in preparation for digestion of a meal. They are supposed to have hay or pasture available at all times. They are not humans.

Why do we want to avoid chemicals such as dewormers in our horses claiming an all natural approach to parasite prevention? Then take down the fence and open the barn door. Natural deworming is letting the horse eat here, defecate there, and be 50 miles away from his last manure pile by the next day. That is how horses do it.

These are a few examples of how we have "humanized" the horse. I am sure you can think of more. Remember though that they are still a horse. Understand that they have similar personalities, that they have a language, they have agendas, they have "horse rules", and they are kept by humans but are not humans.

When I walk into a stall I am very clear with the horse. I am a human and he is a horse. To open up the dialog that leads to communication, I offer my presence as an equal being using the common language of respect. For me to offer him a brochure on the floating process before I start floating would be ridiculous. Even if he could read it, he would not understand the idea. But a horse understands respect and a willingness of a human to first seek to understand their position and then to explain what we are doing.

Watching the slow and gradual look of understanding transform their fearful and tense body into a relaxed and almost sleeping patient as I remove their oral pain still, after 27 years of doing this, almost brings tears to my eyes.

CONCLUSION

This book is a product of my experiences with horses since 1973. I have been blessed to have a job where I experience on average more than 3500 different horses a year. I see people continually make the same avoidable mistakes. It is my goal to bring *The 10 Irrefutable Laws Of Horsemanship* to every horse owner in the world.

I know I will get mixed reviews ranging from brilliant to stupid. It really doesn't matter. What I am looking for is not reviews. I am looking to save at least one life - either man or horse. These laws have saved me repeatedly. Learn them and let them become a part of your life.

BIBLIOGRAPHY

Personality Plus by Florence Littauer
ISBN 10: 0-8007-5445-X
ISBN 978-0-8007-5445-7